DETECTIVE
ACTIVITY
BOOK

Andy Passchier
Gemma Barder

T0016464

ARCTURUS

Are you ready to be a detective? In this book, you will need to find clues and think logically to solve crimes!

ARCTURUS

This edition published in 2024 by Arcturus Publishing Limited
26/27 Bickels Yard, 151–153 Bermondsey Street,
London SE1 3HA

Illustrator: Andy Passchier
Author: Gemma Barder
Editor: Violet Peto
Designer: Ariadne Ward
Managing Editor: Joe Harris
Managing Designer: Georgina Wood

ISBN: 978-1-3988-3607-5
CH010458NT
Supplier 29, Date 1023, PI 00004803

Printed in China

SPOT THE FORGERY!

You have uncovered a pile of banknotes—but they are not all real! Which of these is the forgery? It will look slightly different from all the rest.

FIND THE FOOTPRINT

There has been a robbery at Sleuth City's Central Bank! The only clue the thief left behind was this footprint found at the crime scene. A search of your suspects brings up five possible matches. Use your detective skills to discover who the footprint belongs to.

HACK THE HACKERS

You are trying to hack into a cybercriminal's computer system. Can you find out which symbols are missing from each sequence of yellow symbols on the screen? Fill in the empty squares, then copy them in order at the bottom to reveal the encryption code.

NIGHT AT THE MUSEUM

There has been a break-in at the museum, and some priceless treasure has been stolen! Luckily, these criminals are a bit clumsy and keep dropping jewels as they run away! Make your way through the maze, picking up each jewel as you go.

START

FINISH

THROUGH THE LOOKING GLASS

You have recovered a set of keys from an infamous burglar. Use your detective skills to spot the master key among the decoys.

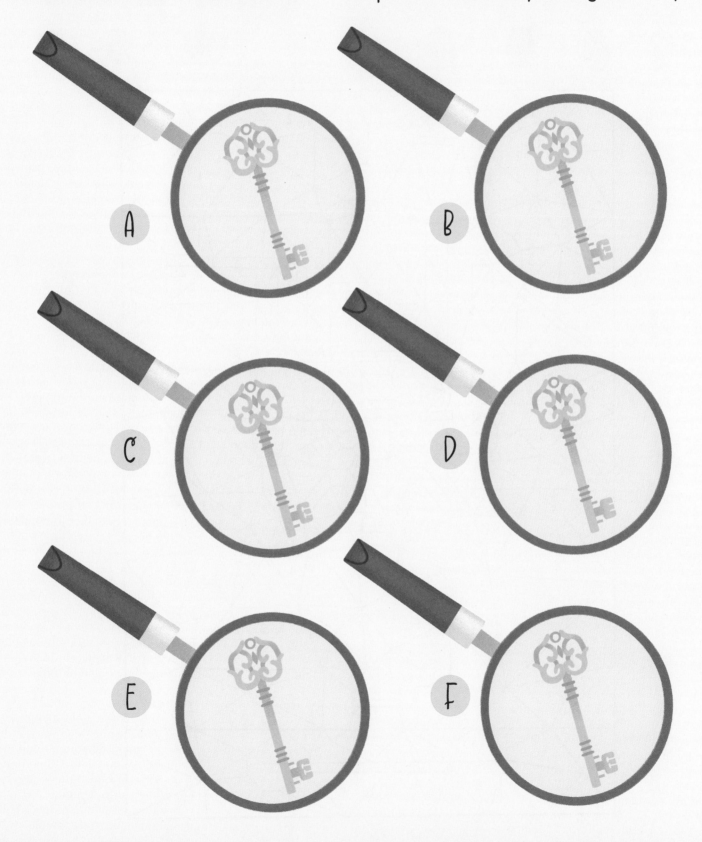

UNCOVER THE TRUTH!

There has been a burglary at the old mansion. Looking at the number code, use your pens or pencils to reveal what has been stolen.

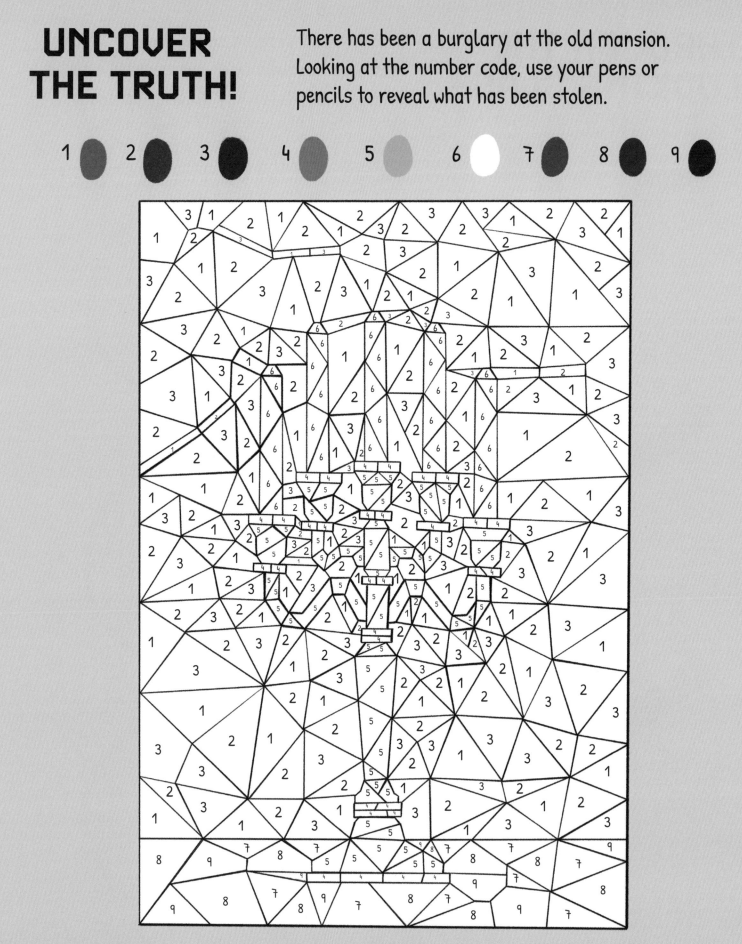

SAFE EQUATIONS

You have recovered three stolen safes with a scrap of paper containing an equation under each one. Figure out the equations from left to right to discover how much money is inside each safe.

4 x 400 – 100

Which safe has the most money in it?

10 x 10 x 9

3000 – 500 + 75

SPOTTED!

You have caught this suspect in the shadows. But who is it? Match the shadow to the criminal to catch your culprit.

CRIME CLUES

When detectives enter a crime scene, they need to take in a lot of information, fast! Take a look at this room for 20 seconds, then see if you can answer all the questions on the next page.

QUESTIONS, QUESTIONS

What can you remember from the crime scene on the previous page?

1. Was the tipped-over chair brown or black?

2. How many plants were there?

3. What did the picture on the wall show?

4. Where were the muddy footprints leading to?

5. How many banknotes were there?

6. Were the curtains pink or purple?

SCENE OF THE CRIME

You are following a series of clues. Can you find out which one comes next in each sequence?

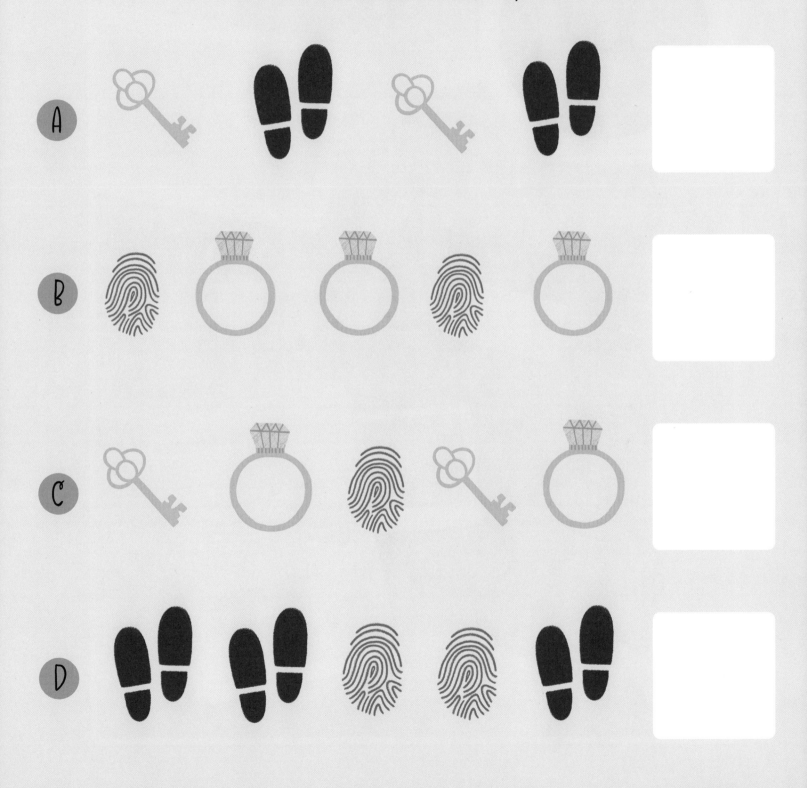

THE DETECTIVE'S DESK

A detective's desk is a very important place. It's where they put clues together, call suspects, and ... eat lunch! Can you find six differences between these two desks?

ON THE CASE!

You need to get to the scene of a crime before the crooks escape! Which is the quickest route?

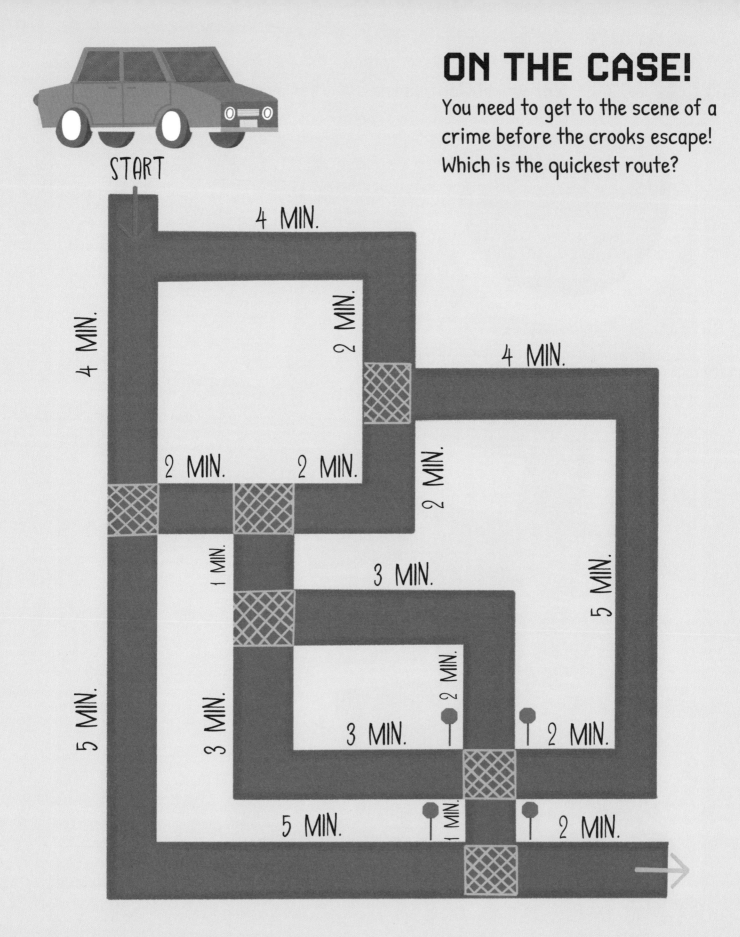

START

4 MIN.

4 MIN.

2 MIN.

4 MIN.

2 MIN.

2 MIN.

2 MIN.

2 MIN.

1 MIN.

3 MIN.

5 MIN.

5 MIN.

3 MIN.

3 MIN.

2 MIN.

2 MIN.

5 MIN.

1 MIN.

2 MIN.

SHREDDED

This map leads straight to the criminal's hideout—but it's been cut up!
Can you put the pieces back together again?

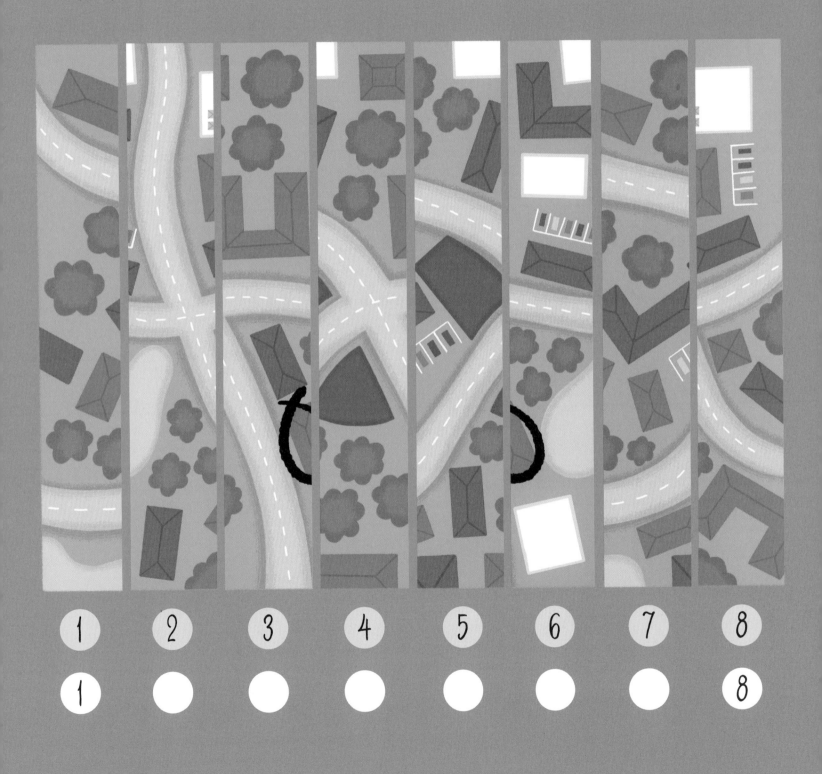

KEYDOKU

The crime boss has hidden important evidence in this vault! To unlock it, you must place one of each type of key into every row, column, and minigrid. Can you complete the grid?

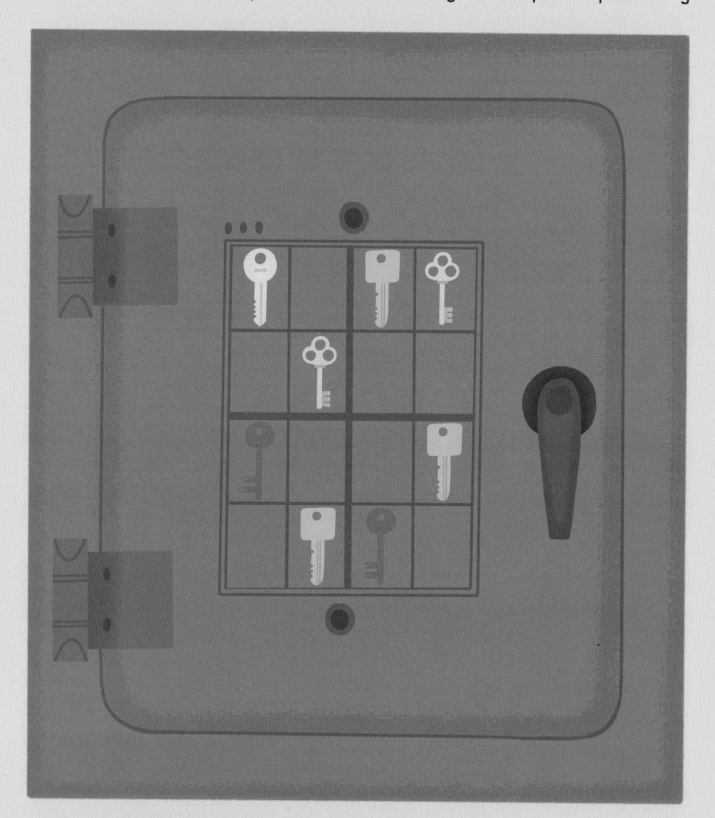

SUITCASE SWITCH

A suitcase containing important documents has gone missing! Read the description to figure out which of these is the missing case.

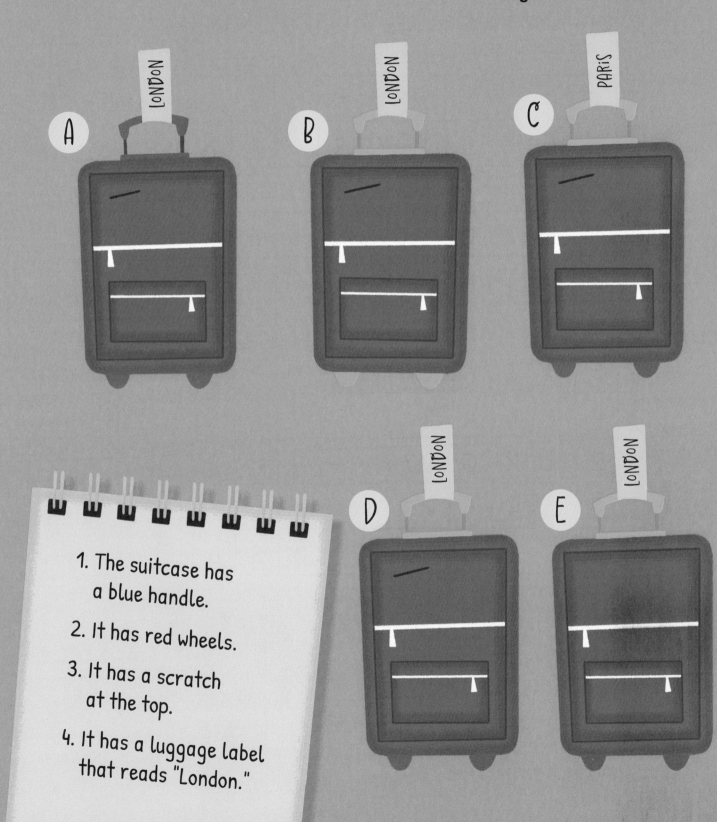

A — LONDON

B — LONDON

C — PARIS

D — LONDON

E — LONDON

1. The suitcase has a blue handle.

2. It has red wheels.

3. It has a scratch at the top.

4. It has a luggage label that reads "London."

CODE NAME CRACKER

The names that appear in the grid are members of a gang. Which two people from the list are not in the gang?

G	O	L	D	F	I	N	G	E	R
M	A	T	B	I	Y	R	R	A	H
L	D	A	S	A	C	O	U	T	T
E	S	J	O	S	T	M	A	E	H
P	H	I	N	E	M	E	A	R	U
Y	S	I	A	D	C	H	S	S	N
E	P	T	A	E	M	B	Y	E	D
R	B	N	A	R	D	E	N	R	E
Z	I	X	C	V	B	N	N	M	R
G	Q	W	E	R	T	Y	A	U	I
F	R	E	D	G	H	Y	D	S	D

Fred
Danny
Gina
Harry
Tallulah
Daisy
Lightning
Thunder
Bates
Goldfinger

20

TAKE A BREAK

Even hard-working detectives need a break sometimes.
Follow the lines to figure out what each detective is having for lunch!

ANCIENT CODES

You have been tailing an infamous gang of art thieves, and you have managed to intercept a secret message. Crack the code to reveal what the gang plans to steal next, and when.

A	B	D	E	G	H	I	M	N	P	R	S	T	X	Y

Write what it says here:

CAPTURE WITH COORDINATES

You have discovered a set of coordinates that lead to the location of some buried stolen goods! Starting at 1A, follow the instructions to decide where to dig:

N3, E2, N3, W1, S2, E2, N1

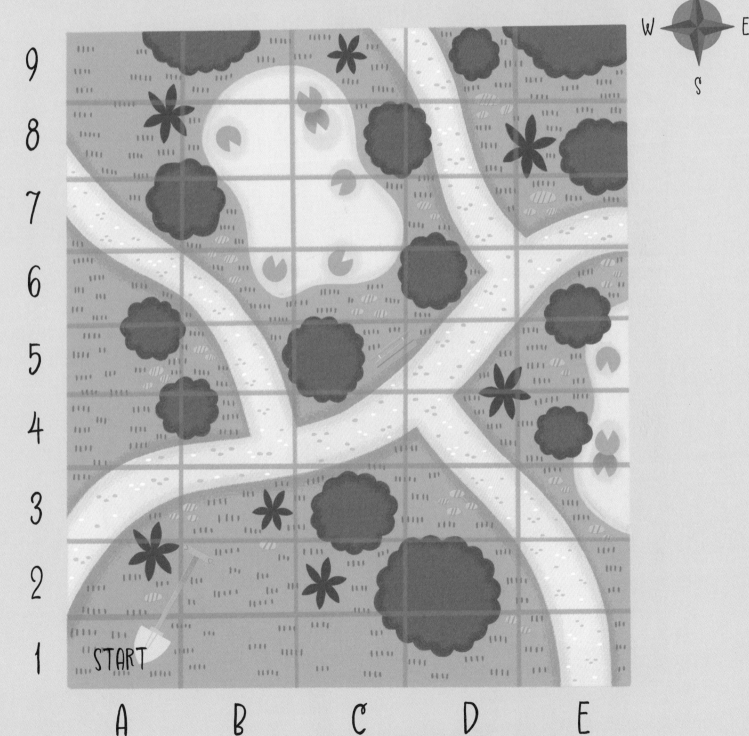

KIT LIST

Unscramble these words to find out what the best detectives keep in their kits at all times.

NPE

NRITGEPFNRI TKI

FDACUSHNF

GINHT IOVISN ESGLGOG

OKNEBOTO

WINDOW WATCH

A devious diamond thief has been tracked to this building, but you don't know which apartment he is in.

Take a look at this shadowy picture taken at the crime scene, and see if you can match it to one of the residents.

STATION SEARCH

The photographs at the top and bottom of these pages show innocent bystanders. Can you find the criminal in the scene?

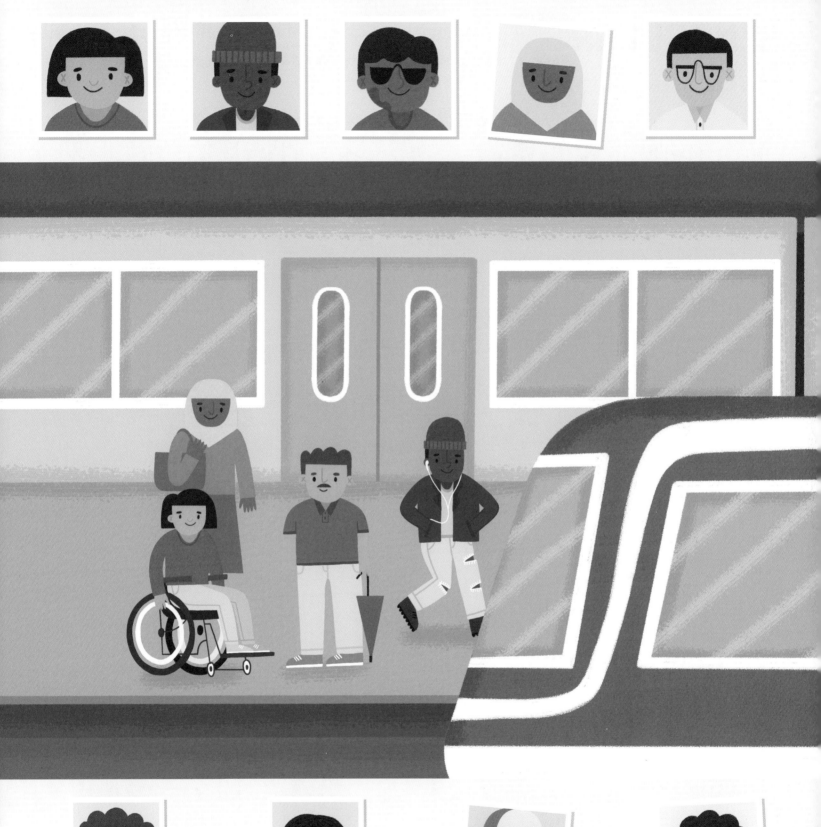

BINOCULAR PILE

Binoculars are an essential part of any detective's kit. How many can you count in this pile?

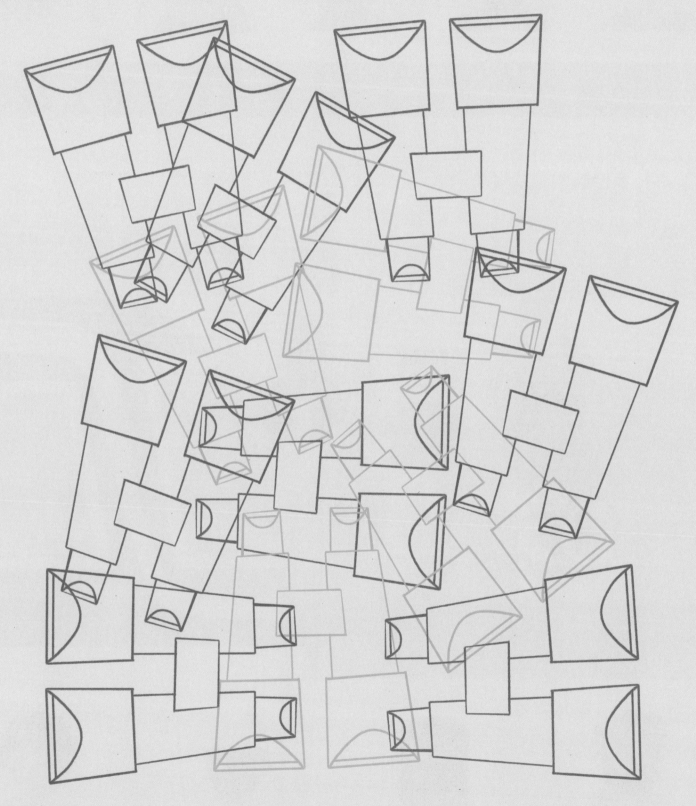

BUSY DAY!

Each of these detectives has solved a case and caught a criminal. Can you match the detective to the person they caught? Clue: Take a close look at the handcuffs!

YOUR NUMBER'S UP!

The answers to each of these equations makes up the suspect's phone number. Use your skills to figure out what it is.

$$5 \times 10 + 5 =$$

$$68 - 14 =$$

$$32 \times 2 =$$

WRITE ON TIME ...

This note was dropped by a criminal running away from a bank robbery! Luckily, you have handwriting samples from the top five bank robbers currently on the run. Can you match the handwriting to the samples below?

NEXT JOB: SATURDAY 3:00 P.M. BOFFINGTON'S BANK

A — ABCDEFG

B — ABCDEFG

C — ABCDEFG

D — ABCDEFG

E — ABCDEFG

ON THE CHASE!

Quick! Don't let the getaway driver escape into the crowd.
Take a look at each car carefully to find the odd one out—that's the car to chase!

MONEY BAGS

There's been a robbery at Sleuth City Bank.
Each of these bags of money should contain $100.

Two bank notes have been stolen from each one. Remember, banknotes come in $1, $5, $10, $20, and $50. Can you figure out which banknotes have been stolen?

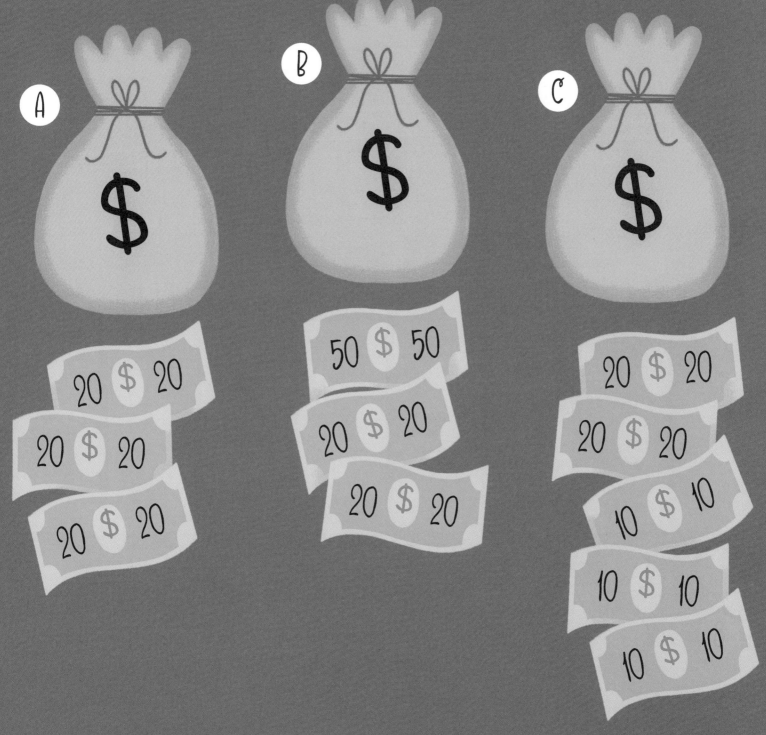

SNOW JOKE

Secret formulas have been stolen from this laboratory, and the thief has tampered with the CCTV image to prevent you from tracking them down. Use your detective skills to put this CCTV picture back together and find out which direction the criminal went!

GADGET SEARCH

You are packing your case ready for your next assignment. Which case do all the items fit into?

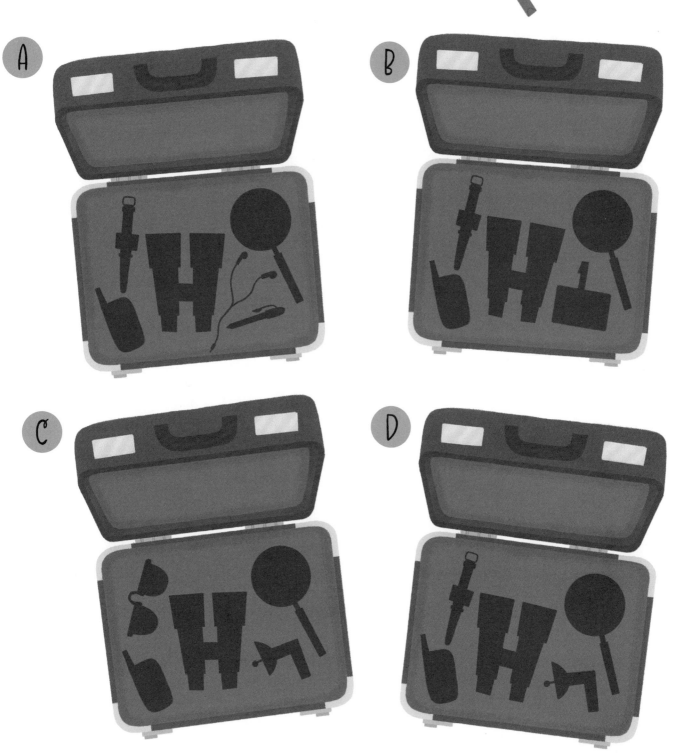

NO STONE UNTURNED

There is stolen evidence behind this door! The key is under one of the paving stones. To find out which one, you must follow these secret coordinates starting at A1:

N5, E3, S4, W1, N2

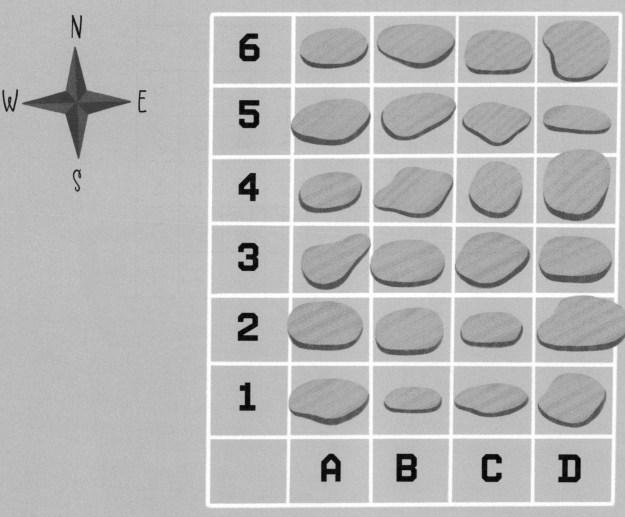

MISSING!
PUPPY ON THE LOOSE

The owners of a missing puppy last saw him scampering into a spooky old house! Can you track him through the maze?

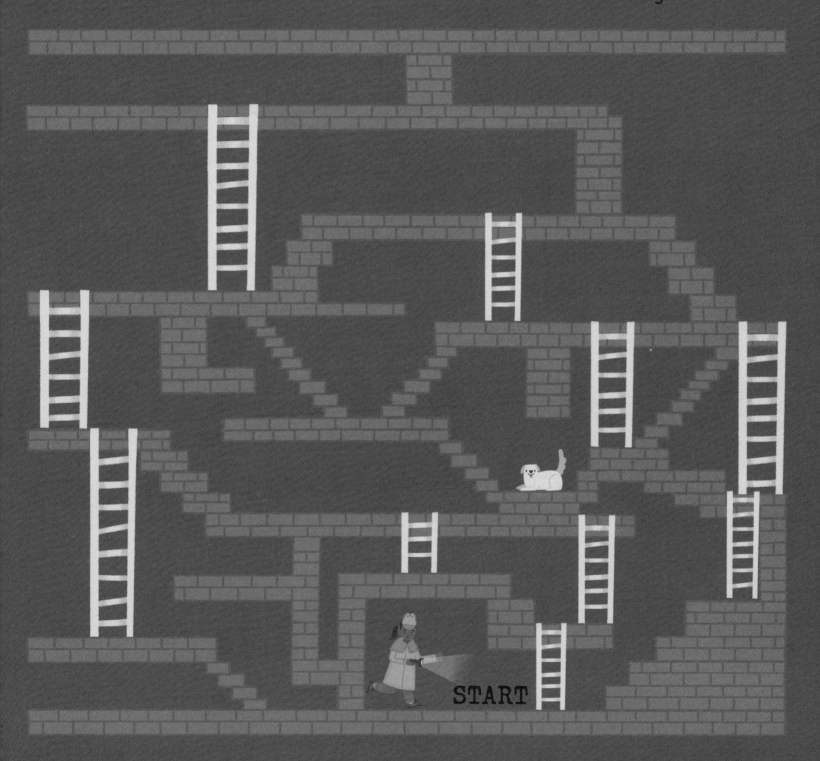

START

STOLEN CUPCAKES!

The pictures on the left were taken before and after
a plate of delicious cupcakes was stolen!

One of these three
suspects took them!
Can you find out who
the cupcake thief is?

A

B

C

DOTS TO SPOT

A clever gang of thieves is on the run. Connect the dots to reveal where the gang is hiding.

DESK TIDY SUDOKU

To keep a clear head, detectives need a tidy desk to work from. Sort each of these items so that they only appear once in each column, row, and minigrid.

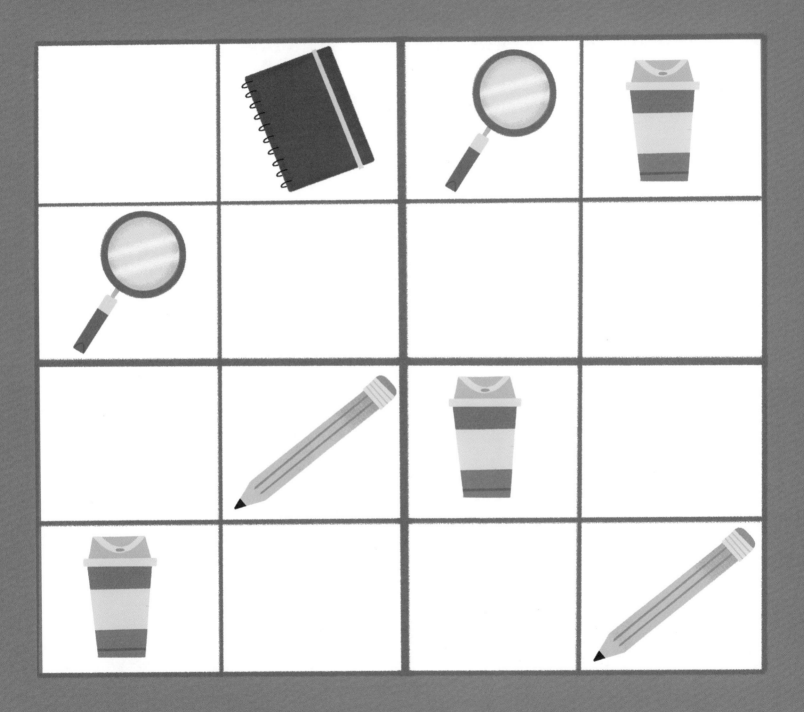

A HUNGRY HIT!

You have received a coded tip-off revealing the whereabouts of some stolen jewels from a recent heist. Decipher the foodie code to find out what has been hidden and where.

Foodie Code

ARE	OVEN	IN	PIZZA	EMERALDS	DIAMONDS
COFFEE	BEHIND	THE	DUMPLING	FRIDGE	SHOP

DUMPLINGS

PIZZA

COFFEE

PHOTOFIT

A witness spotted someone stealing all the Christmas lights from the town tree. Can you help them remember what the suspect looked like? Choose the eyes, nose, and mouth that fit into the shapes on the photofit.

CAR CHASE!

Quick! Time to jump in your undercover police vehicle and FOLLOW THAT CAR! Follow the lines, and count the minutes as you go to find the quickest route!

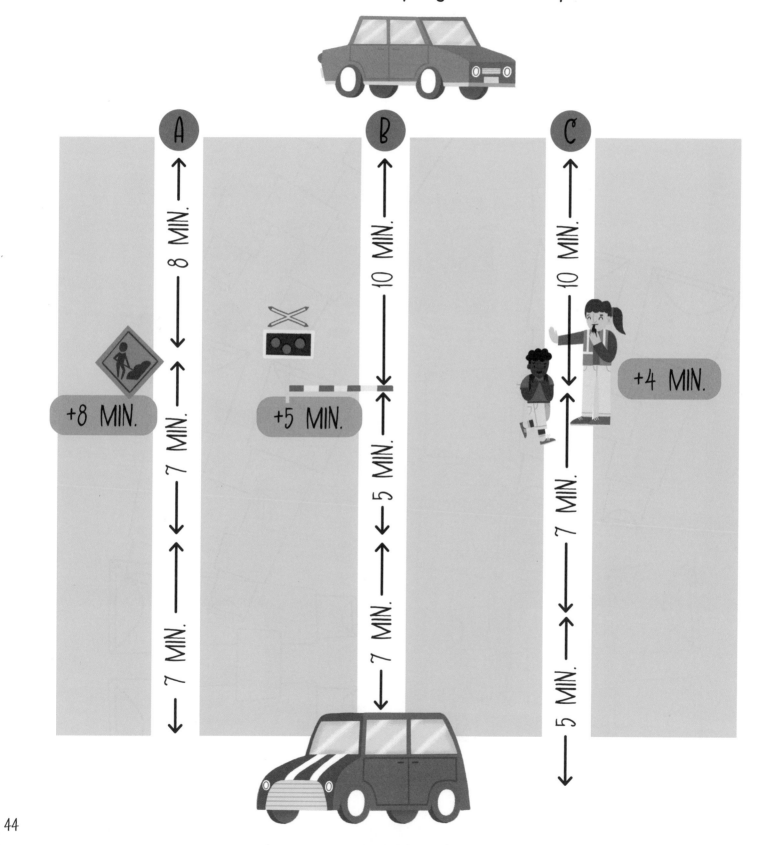

MYSTERY MESSAGE

A gang of art thieves have abandoned their hideout and destroyed all the evidence!

You discover a shredded picture at the scene. Put the strips back together in the correct order to reveal the location of their next target.

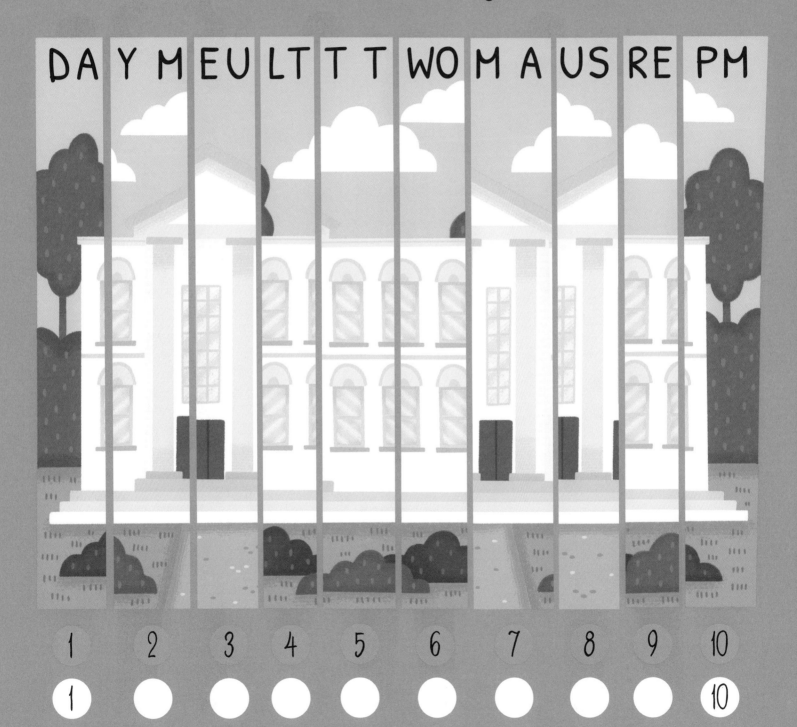

1   2   3   4   5   6   7   8   9   10

① ○ ○ ○ ○ ○ ○ ○ ○ ⑩

MYSTERY MONEY

A suitcase full of bags of money has been found after a robbery at the supermarket, but some of the money is still missing. Figure out what is missing from each bag by completing the sequences.

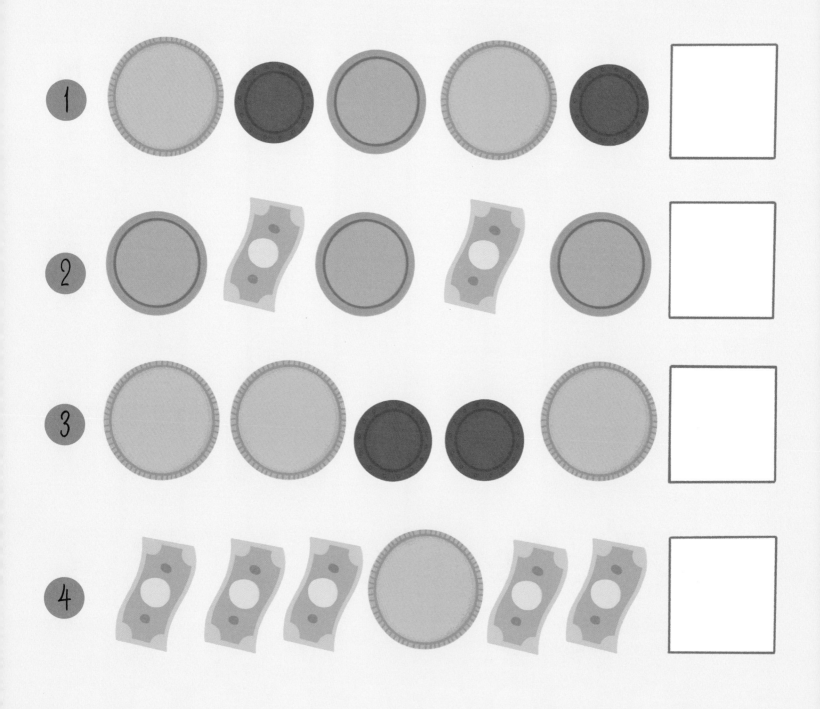

AIRPORT RUNAWAY

You have received a tip-off that a notorious cybercriminal is at the airport. Can you catch her and seize her laptop before she escapes from the country?
This is what you know about her:

She wears glasses.

Her hair is brown.

She carries her laptop in a blue shoulder bag.

CRACKED CASE

There has been a robbery at the docks! Luckily, a witness captured an image of the two criminals before they escaped. Unfortunately, the witness dropped his phone, and the screen smashed.

Can you find the missing pieces to put the screen back together again?

WHAT A LINEUP!

1   2   3   4   5

A notorious forger has been brought in for
questioning, but you need to look closely to find
the right man! Look at the suspects for 20 seconds
paying close attention to head shapes and facial
features. Then turn the page to identify the faker.

CAN YOU SPOT THE FORGER?

Look at this surveillance picture of the forger.
Can you remember which one he is from the lineup on the
previous page? Try not to peek back!

ZOO ESCAPE!

Last night, someone broke into the Sleuth City Zoo and stole one of the most popular animals! Following the chart, shade in the shapes to find out which animal was taken.

1 2 3 4 5 6 7 8 9

ALL ABOUT THE PRINTS

A thief has left fingerprints all over the counter after breaking into the bakery. Take a close look at the fingerprint in the yellow folder, then see if you can match it to a suspect.

SHOE SHUFFLE

A pickpocket has been stealing from the local gym. A witness says he only saw the shoes of the criminal before he sprinted off. Can you spot the criminal's shoes from the witness's notes?

A

B

C

D

E

1. The shoes have black soles.
2. The laces were undone.
3. Each shoe had five yellow stars.
4. The shoes had a red toe.

SMASHING HIT

These criminals decided that their best escape was through a wall! Can you match each runaway to the hole they made?

GLITTERING HAUL

This pile of rings, necklaces, and bracelets was taken from a notorious jewel thief! Now that the thief is safely behind bars, all that's left is to match the jewels with their owners.

Take a look at the pile, and cross each one off as you find it. Which item is missing from the hoard?

Miss Featherington:
5 ruby rings and a sapphire necklace ○

Mr. Dazzle:
3 gold bracelets and a pair of cufflinks ○

Mrs. Hamilton-Smyth:
2 emerald rings, a pearl ring, and a diamond-studded necklace ○

WOODLAND HIDEOUT

Deep in the forest, you have found a secret hideout, filled with money bags, equipment, and plans! You'll need to work fast to gather the evidence and take pictures of everything on the list in the panel. Check off the items as you find them.

☐ Folded map

☐ Money bags

☐ Blueprint

☐ Masks

☐ Bulletin board

☐ Shovel

YOUR DETECTIVE NAME!

You've been solving puzzles just like a real detective, so now it's time to discover your name! Check the charts below to find it out.

YOUR EYES ARE ...

BLUE	Investigator
BROWN	Officer
GREEN	Detective
AMBER	Inspector
MIXED	Agent

YOUR BIRTH MONTH is ...

JANUARY	Sparky
FEBRUARY	Sharp
MARCH	Snooper
APRIL	Thunderbolt
MAY	Witty
JUNE	Sleuth
JULY	Wily
AUGUST	Brainiac
SEPTEMBER	Onthecase
OCTOBER	Cluedo
NOVEMBER	Catcher
DECEMBER	Gotcha

LOST IN THE TOWN

You have managed to secretly place a tracker on a bank robber!

Read the clues sent by the tracker, to discover where the suspect is hiding. Mark an X on the map showing the location.

1. They are south of the north pond.

2. They are west of the church.

3. They are north of the pizza place.

4. They are east of the school.

ART HEIST

A painting has gone missing from the museum. Take a close look at an excerpt from the museum's guide book below to figure out which one was taken.

SOME VERY OLD AND IMPORTANT ITALIAN RENAISSANCE PAINTINGS

PORTRAIT OF MARCO DE CAPPUCCINO, 1434

GIOVANNA DA BOLOGNESE, 1516

WOMAN WITH PEARL NECKLACE, 1501

SELF-PORTRAIT OF GIORGIO BOMBINI, 1509

WATCH OUT!

There is a sale of designer watches at the auction house. But fraudsters have entered a fake designer watch into the sale! Can you spot the fake?

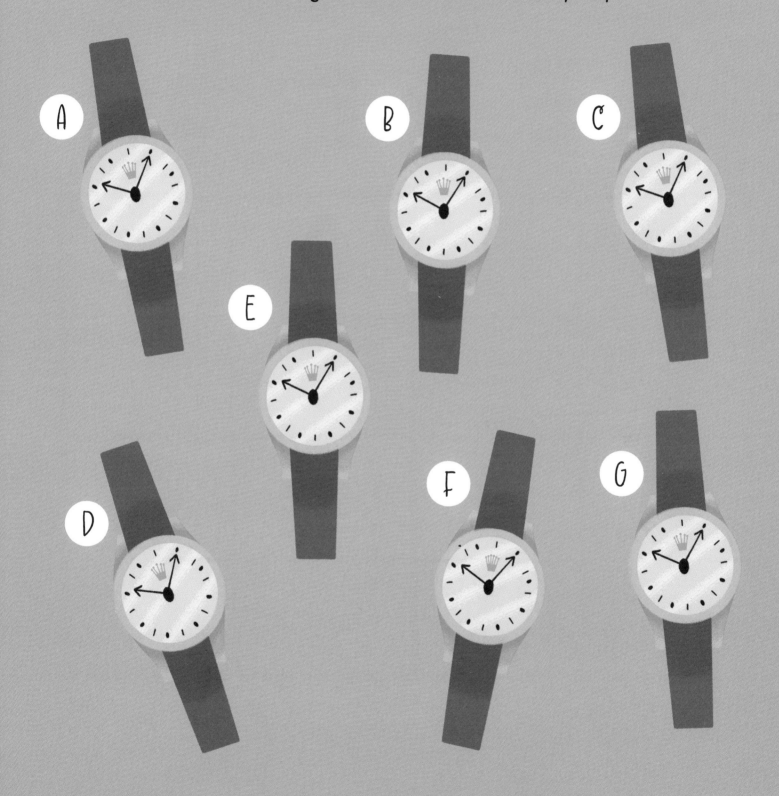

JEWEL COUNT!

You have found a stash of stolen gems and Lady Bingley believes they might be the gems that were stolen from her many weeks ago. She will only know once they have been sorted properly.

Can you sort them so that each gem fits only once in every row, column, and minigrid?

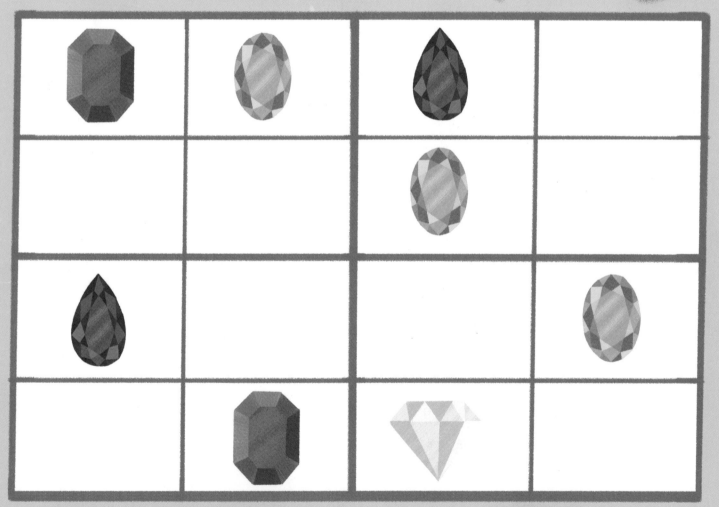

MISSING KITTY

You have been hired to find this family's missing cat.
Read their description to figure out which cat is theirs.

ENTER THE WEB

You are on the tail of a cybercriminal. Find your way through the lines of code to hack into his computer and catch him!

OPEN CASE

Each of these briefcases contains top secret documents. Solve the equations, and write your answers in the squares to crack the combination codes and open the cases!

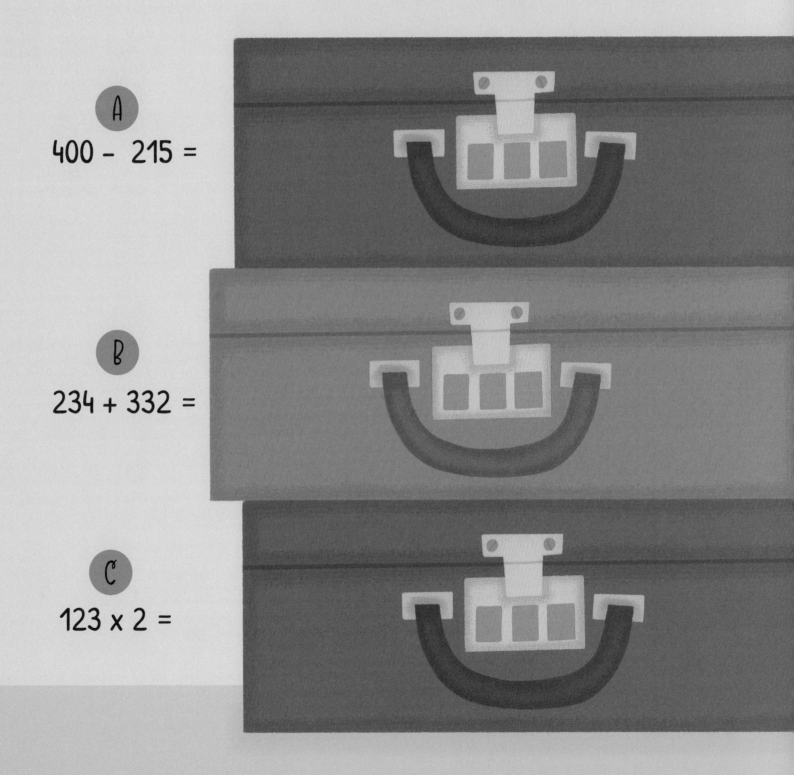

A

400 − 215 =

B

234 + 332 =

C

123 x 2 =

INTERNATIONAL SEARCH

You have been chasing criminal mastermind Agneta Theroux across the globe, but she is always one step ahead of you! You know that she is en route to one of the destinations listed below—which one? The correct destination is the only one that is missing from the grid. That is where you will find her!

Paris	Berlin	Tokyo	Canberra
London	Beijing	Washington	Oslo

Q	D	F	G	H	Y	C	W	Z	X
A	O	Y	K	O	T	G	A	T	Y
B	H	J	M	K	S	D	S	W	E
B	E	I	J	I	N	G	H	M	B
A	T	I	L	D	N	S	I	A	E
S	O	O	U	O	I	T	N	E	R
S	L	A	D	R	E	J	G	O	L
E	S	N	A	H	I	N	T	E	I
H	O	P	A	R	S	H	O	S	N
L	A	P	T	E	M	B	N	E	R

WHEELY BIG TROUBLE

Your motorcycle has been vandalized by the very gang you are trying to catch! Using an old photograph for reference, find all the missing pieces, then get on their trail!

RIVER PANIC

You have followed a suspect all the way to a river.

Starting at 10, link the numbers and symbols on the stepping stones to find the quickest route of equations. The equation with the lowest total will get you across in the fastest time.

START

10   x

8   4

12   –   9

+   1   =

FINISH

DRAW THE SUSPECT

As a top detective, you need to be able to remember the faces of the criminals you are tracking! Take a look at this old mugshot of infamous cat-napper Josephine Florent, then turn the page to see how much you remember.

JOSEPHINE FLORENT

DRAW THE SUSPECT

Draw a picture of Josephine Florent on the noticeboard so that all your colleagues know who to look out for!

CRYPTIC CLUES!

Solve these riddles, then match them to the pictures. Enter the numbers for each riddle in the correct order to crack the password and hack into the criminal's laptop!

What has hands and a face, but can't hold anything or smile?

What gets shorter the older it gets?

What travels, but stays in the same place?

What gets wetter the more it dries?

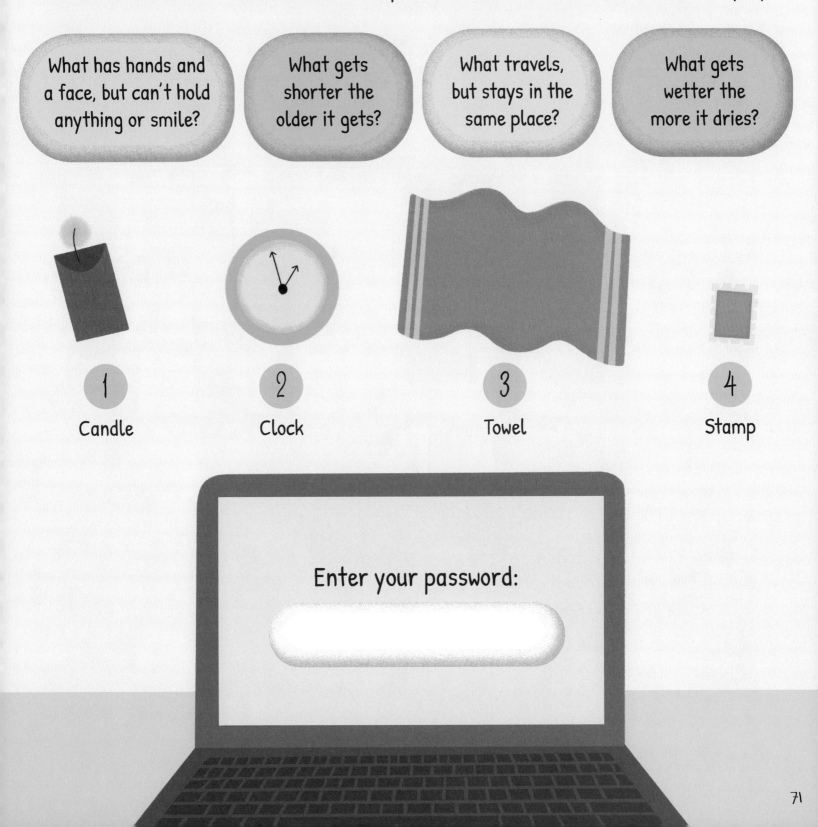

1 Candle

2 Clock

3 Towel

4 Stamp

Enter your password:

PANIC IN THE LIBRARY!

Take a look at these photographs taken before and after a break-in at Sleuth City Library.

The most valuable books have their title on the spine. One is missing, can you figure out which it is?

PIECING HISTORY TOGETHER

This old picture holds the key to your next mystery! The thieves have written the name of the next place they are going to burgle, but it has been torn into pieces. Put it back together again to stop the crime!

1. KET
2. EET
3. MA STR
4. ON R
5. BAK
6. ERY

CAUGHT RED-HANDED!

This criminal's hand was spotted on CCTV as it reached into the rare items cabinet in the antique shop! Take a look at the hands of five different suspects—which one matches the CCTV picture perfectly?

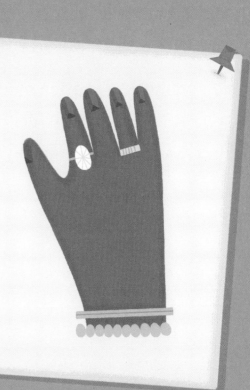

1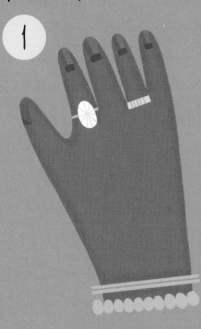

2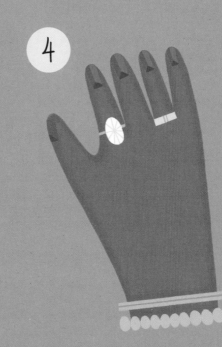

5

3

4

EVERY OTHER WORD

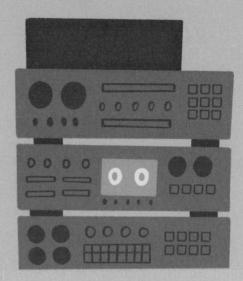

This automatic dictation machine took down an important witness statement after an attempted robbery. But it has malfunctioned and added in lots of words that shouldn't be there!

Cross out every second word to get the correct statement.

I rabbit saw gift the flag gang kite run peas away telephone toward monkey the gym swimming camera pool. Bob They giraffe were nets all umbrella dressed plug in sponge black.

PAPER AND PENS

An important part of a detective's kit is a trusty notepad and pen.
How many of each can you see in this pile?

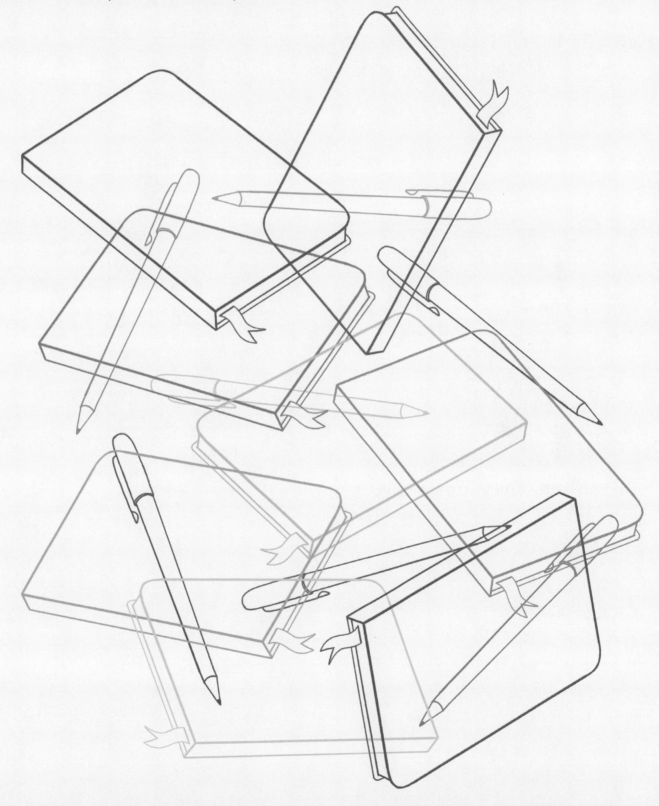

SLICED STATEMENT

There has been a break-in at your office, and an important witness statement has been ripped up! Can you put the pieces back together again? Match the beginnings and endings of each sentence by drawing a line between them.

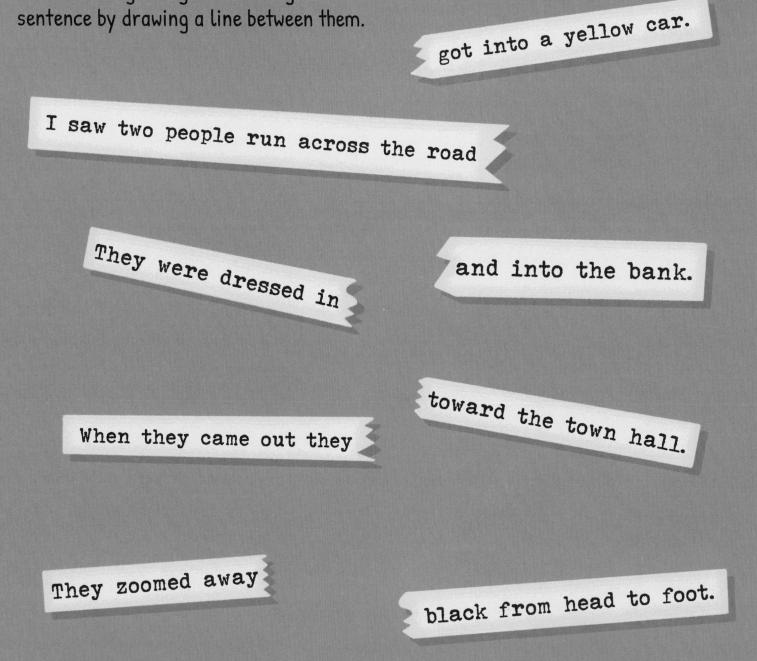

got into a yellow car.

I saw two people run across the road

They were dressed in

and into the bank.

When they came out they

toward the town hall.

They zoomed away

black from head to foot.

UNDERGROUND OPERATION

You are on the lookout for a very tricky criminal who is great at disguising themselves! They are in this CCTV image, but which passenger could it be? Take a look at this scene for 20 seconds, then turn the page.

TUESDAY 06:34:04

UNDERGROUND OPERATION

This CCTV picture was taken 20 seconds after the first one! Can you spot the sneaky suspect in a new disguise?

TUESDAY 06:34:24

NIGHT SHIFT

This detective is working late at the station. Which of these shadows matches her desk perfectly?

A

B

C

D

E

ALL IN THE LETTERS

You have received a ransom note in several torn up pieces. Can you piece it back together to reveal the message?

DROPPeD In

Our mONeY oR

AMuLET

THe GoLdEN

IT GeTs

We HAVe

AT MiDnight

GIVE Us

The OCeaN

Use this space to solve the puzzle:

LISTENING IN

You have bugged the apartment of a prime suspect, but your wires have become tangled. Follow the wire from your listening device to find out which room you are connected to.

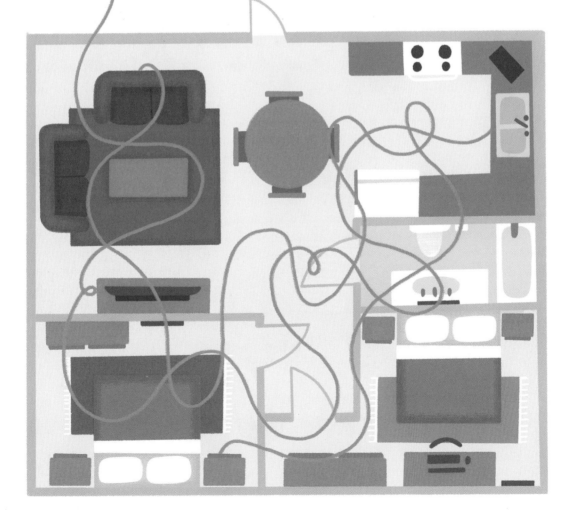

MARKET MISHAPS

You have been given a tip-off that a criminal is lurking in the town market. It's very busy, and you don't want to alarm anyone. Take a look at the descriptions of the suspect, and see if you can spot them in the crowd.

CASE CLOSED

A case has been closed, and now all that is left to do is sort out the paperwork. Put each of these files into the cabinet in order. There should be one in each row, column, and minigrid.

MISSING MAMMALS

There has been a break-in at the zoo, and some of the animals have gone missing. Unscramble the letters on each of these signs to figure out which animals have been stolen.

NOLI

TGIER

MKEONY

GFRIAFE

PNDAA

SALWUR

BUON APPETITO!

You are on the hunt for two suspects inside this busy Italian restaurant! But where have they gone? Find your way through without disturbing any customers.

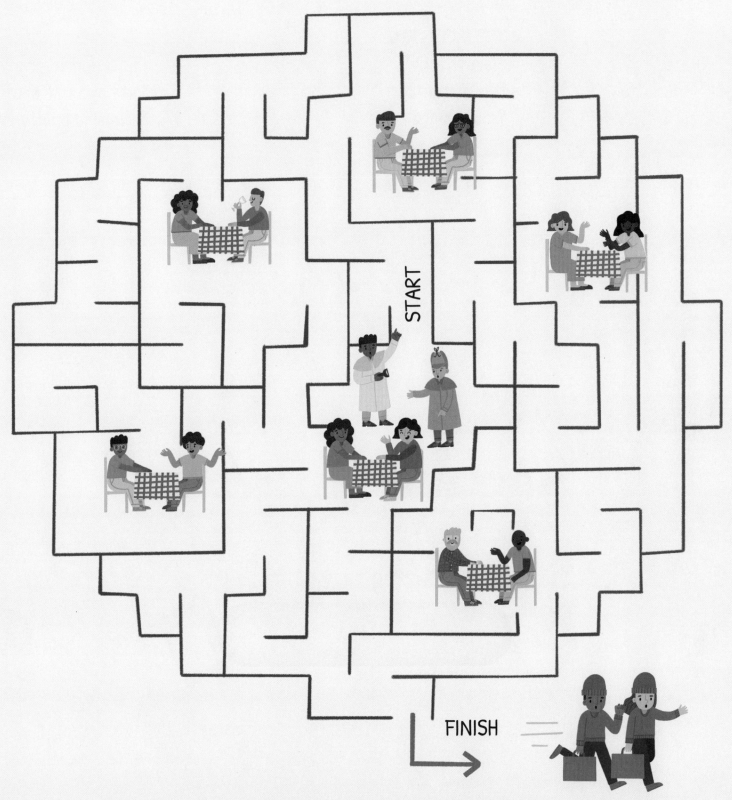

START

FINISH

EVIDENCE TRAIL

There has been a break-in at the diamond store. Gather all the evidence left at the scene, and arrange them in the correct sequences.

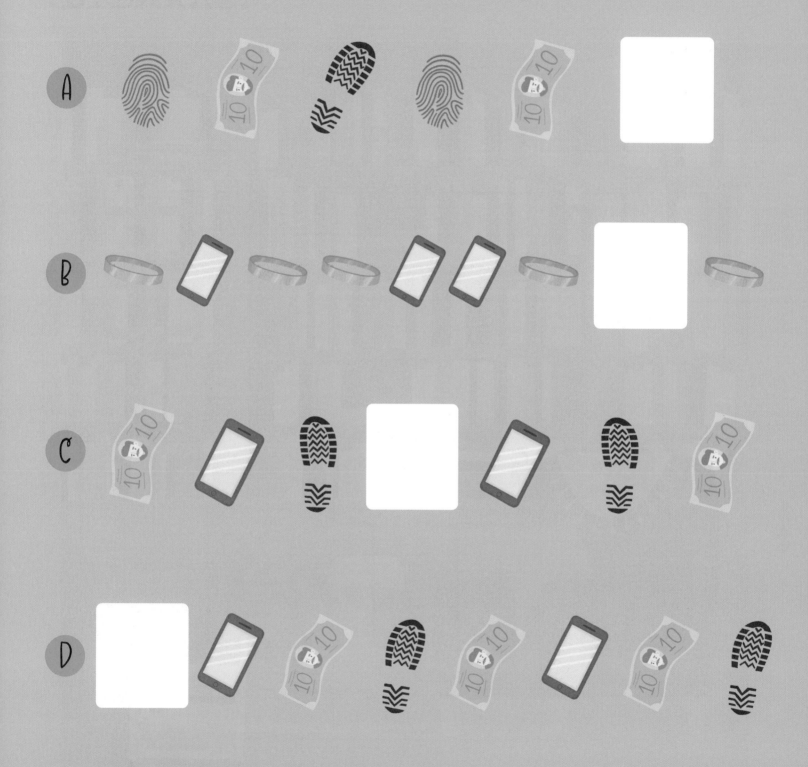

PARTY TIME!

Well done—you have solved all the cases in this book! It's time to celebrate with your fellow detectives. Can you put this scene of a party back together?

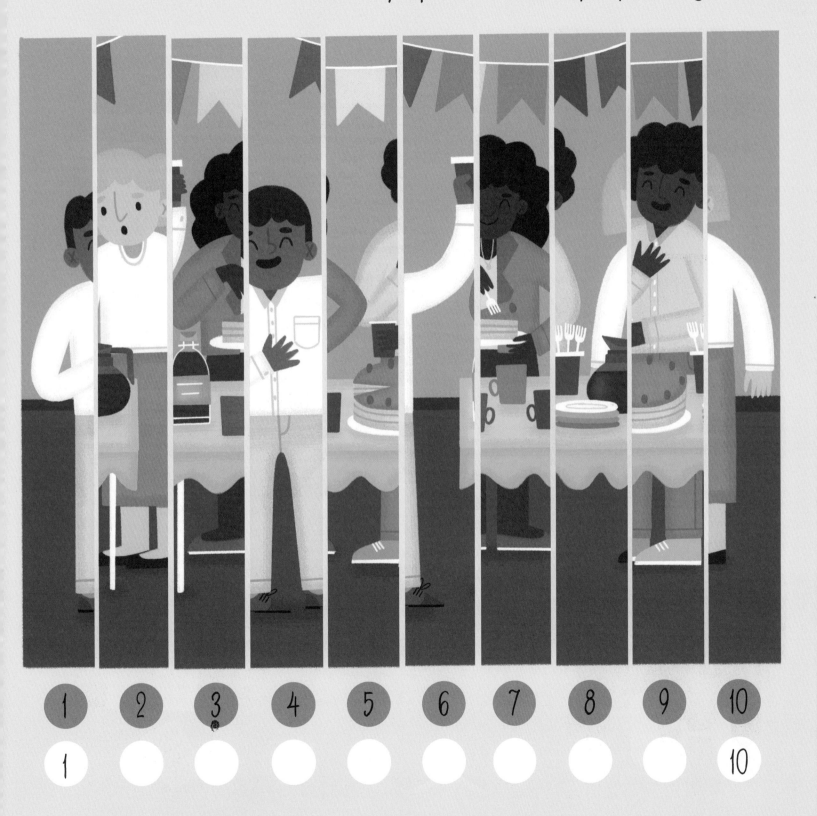

1 2 3 4 5 6 7 8 9 10

1   10

Page 3
E is the forged banknote.

Page 4
The footprint belongs to suspect B.

Page 5

Page 6

Page 7
D is the faulty magnifying glass.

Page 8

A candelabra has been stolen from the old mansion.

Page 9
Safe A—4 x 400 - 100 = 1,500
Safe B—10 x 10 x 9 = 900
Safe C—3,000 - 500 + 75 = 2,575
Safe C has the most money in it.

Page 10
Suspect B is the criminal that matches the shadow.

Pages 11–12
1. The tipped-over chair was brown.
2. There were 3 plants.
3. The picture on the wall was of a cat.
4. The muddy footprints were leading to the window.
5. There were 3 banknotes.
6. The curtains were pink.

Page 13

Pages 14–15

Page 16

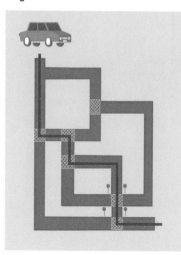

The quickest route takes 15 minutes.

Page 17

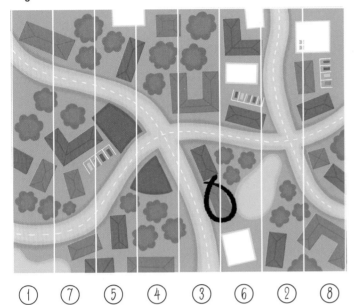

① ⑦ ⑤ ④ ③ ⑥ ② ⑧

Page 18

Page 19
Suitcase D is the missing suitcase.

Page 20

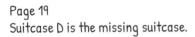

Tallulah and Lightning are not in the gang.

Page 21
This is what each detective is having for lunch:

Page 22
SAPPHIRE SPHINX
MIDNIGHT

Page 23
You should dig in D6.

Page 24

Page 25

91

Pages 26–27

Page 28
There are 12 binoculars in the pile.

Page 29
1–B
2–A
3–C

Page 30
The suspect's phone number is 555464.

Page 31
The handwriting matches suspect B's sample.

Page 32
Car D is the odd one out. That's the one to chase!

Page 33
2 $20 banknotes have been stolen from bag A.
2 $5 banknotes have been stolen from bag B.
A $10 and a $20 banknote have been stolen from bag C.

Page 34

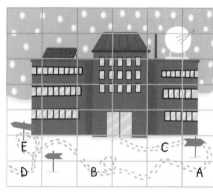

The criminal went in the direction of the park.

Page 35
All the items fit into case D.

Page 36
The key is under the rock in C4.

Page 37

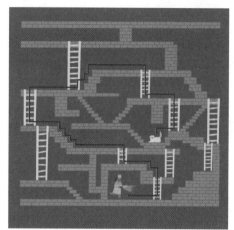

Pages 38–39
Suspect A is the cupcake thief.
What are the clues? He left shoeprints and he has pink icing on his mouth!

Page 40

The gang is hiding at the circus.

Page 41

Page 42
DIAMONDS ARE IN THE PIZZA OVEN

Page 43

Page 44
Route A: 30 minutes; Route B: 27 minutes; Route C: 26 minutes
Route C is the quickest route.

Page 45

DALTREY MUSEUM AT TWO PM

① ④ ⑨ ② ⑧ ③ ⑦ ⑤ ⑥ ⑩

Page 46

1.   2.   3.   4.

Page 47

Page 48

Pages 49—50
Suspect 3 is the forger.

Page 51

Page 52
The fingerprint belongs to suspect A.

Page 53
E is the pair of shoes that belong to the pickpocket.

Page 54

Page 55
Miss Featherington:
5 ruby rings and a
sapphire necklace

Mr. Dazzle:
3 gold bracelets and a
pair of cufflinks

Mrs. Hamilton-Smyth:
2 emerald rings and
a diamond-studded
necklace

Mrs. Hamilton-Smyth's pearl ring is missing from the hoard.

Pages 56-57

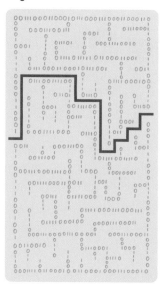

Page 59

Page 60
Woman with Pearl Necklace was taken from the museum.

Page 61
Watch F is the fake.

Page 62

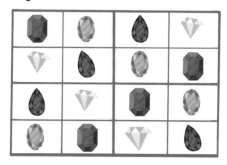

Page 63
Cat D belongs to the family.

Page 64

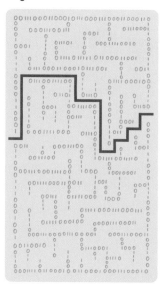

Page 65
A. 400 − 215 = 185
B. 234 + 332 = 566
C. 123 x 2 = 246

Page 66

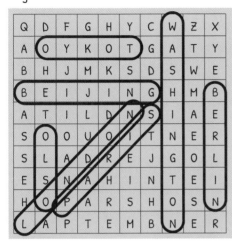

Canberra is her next destination.

Page 67

Page 68

10 x 4 − 12 + 1 = 29 is the fastest route.

Page 71
The password is: 2 1 4 3

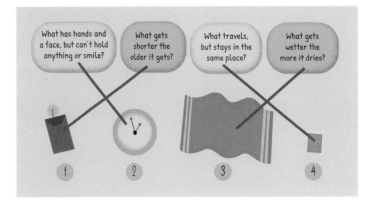

Pages 72–73
The rare book that was stolen was How to Speak Dog.

Page 74

The message is: BAKERY ON MARKET STREET

Page 75
Hand 5 is the perfect match.

Page 76
The correct statement: I saw the gang run away toward the swimming pool. They were all dressed in black.

Page 77
There are 7 pens and 8 notepads.

Page 78

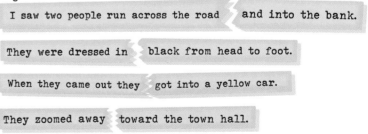

I saw two people run across the road and into the bank.

They were dressed in black from head to foot.

When they came out they got into a yellow car.

They zoomed away toward the town hall.

Pages 79–80

Page 81
Silhouette C matches the detective's desk perfectly.

Page 82

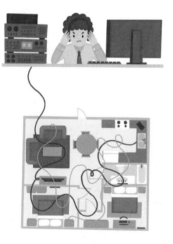

Page 83
Your listening device is connected to the kitchen.

Page 84

Page 85

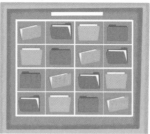

Page 86
These are the animals that need to be found:
LION
TIGER
MONKEY
GIRAFFE
PANDA
WALRUS

Page 87

Page 88

A.    B.   C.   D.

Page 89

① ④ ⑥ ③ ⑦ ⑤ ⑨ ⑧ ② ⑩